HOW TO DECLUTTER YOUR DIGITAL LIFE AND
RECLAIM YOUR ATTENTION

ONE
CLICK
AWAY

SCOTT ALLAN

One Click Away

The 7-Day Digital Decluttering Method

More Bestselling Titles From Scott Allan

Empower Your Thoughts

Drive Your Destiny

Relaunch Your Life

Do the Hard Things First

Undefeated

No Punches Pulled

Fail Big

Built for Stealth

Check out the complete collection of books and training here:

www.scottallanbooks.com

One Click Away

**The 7-Day Digital
Decluttering Method**

*How to Overcome the Digital
Hoarding Addiction and
Reclaim Your Attention*

By Scott Allan

https://www.scottallanpublishing.com/

Contents

A Message from the Author

Dear Reader,

As you hold 'One Click Away,' you're not just holding a book; you're holding a journey towards digital tranquility. I wrote this book because, like many, I found myself lost in the digital labyrinth of endless notifications and online clutter. This journey began with a simple question: How can we reclaim our focus in a world that's constantly vying for our attention?

This book is for you—the digital wanderers, the productivity seekers, and those yearning for a more mindful digital existence. My goal is to guide you through the art of digital decluttering, helping you create a space that nurtures focus, creativity, and peace.

As you delve into these pages, expect to uncover practical strategies for managing digital distractions, insights into digital minimalism, and techniques to enhance your everyday focus. It's not just about turning off notifications; it's about redefining your digital habits to serve your well-being.

Writing 'One Click Away' was a transformative experience. It challenged my perceptions and deepened my understanding of our digital interactions. I hope it does the same for you—inspiring a change that goes beyond the screen.

Thank you for joining me on this journey. Together, let's embrace the quiet, focus-filled life that's just one click away.

With gratitude,

Scott Allan

January 12th, 2024

Introduction

Do you often feel overwhelmed when you switch from one tab to another on your laptop?

Do you feel that the digital world has completely taken over your life, preventing you from doing your job well?

Do you often feel distracted and unsure of what to do every time you open your computer?

Do you often get sidetracked from important tasks or lost in a sea of data, applications, documents, bookmarks, and what-nots stored on your digital devices?

If your answer to any of these questions is a resounding yes, you need to go on a digital cleanse. *One Click Away* is your formula for taking control of your digital life so you can be less stressed and happier.

Yes, digital decluttering is what you need to free yourself from the stress, overwhelm and distractions that eat away at your productivity.

This is where *One Click Away* comes in.

One Click Away is about overcoming the addiction to digital hoarding and decluttering your digital data across all devices, cloud storage, and applications.

This book walks you through the Digital Decluttering Method and teaches you step-by-step how to clean up and eliminate the data that has taken up a lot of space in your digital and mental space.

In One Click Away, you will come clean, realize if you are a digital junkie, what kind of digital junkie you are, and how to dismantle the chaos of your digital environment.

Why One Click Away?

You are always *One Click Away* from your next online purchase, your next free download, or your next software, app, or eBook purchase. One Click Away is all that stands between you and digital chaos.

Before you click that download or purchase button, learn to think things through in three easy steps.

Who is this book for?

This book is for anyone who feels overwhelmed by the documents, videos, photos, emails, applications, and other media that consume their daily lives.

I've written this book for someone - like you - who has begun to recognize the dangers of "digital noise" but feels helpless about how to live in today's world without experiencing digital overload.

The book will also be very helpful to anyone who wants to develop a system for dealing with and managing the information they actually want. Ultimately, the book will help you reclaim the time you have wasted on digital clutter and give you strategies to maximize the time you spend in the digital world.

How this book can help you

One Click Away can help you declutter your digital life in many ways:

- It will help you understand the different types of digital clutter you are hoarding, allowing you to identify the types of clutter.

- It provides simple, step-by-step guidelines that teach you the art of gradually removing digital clutter.

- It helps you identify what really matters to you.

- It allows you to reduce the undue stress and pressure that digital hoarding places on you.

- It helps you understand your data hoarding type, so you can take appropriate steps to streamline things accordingly.

- Provides insight into how digital clutter is weighing you down and negatively impacting your life.

- Encourages you on why you need to start cleaning up your digital life.

- Guides you through an 11-step approach to reclaiming your productivity.

- It talks about the places where digital clutter can accumulate, so you can effectively clean them up.

- It helps you understand the do's and don'ts of digital decluttering and prepares you with everything you need to do it right.

As you progress through this book, you will find yourself taking incremental steps that will help you get rid of all the annoying digital clutter you have accumulated over the years.

What is Digital Decluttering?

Digital decluttering is simply arranging or organizing your content on your devices (phone, tablet, computer) and accounts by deleting the apps or files you no longer use.

Organizing your digital workspace through decluttering has become essential because it frees us from undue stress, helps us streamline our work, and encourages us to focus on the important tasks that increase our productivity.

As residents of the 21st century, we have vast amounts of information to use and store.

Because information is so accessible, we often get caught up in all the data, apps, tools, and massive amounts of information in the form of videos and PDFs, resulting in a huge amount of digital clutter that only overwhelms us.

Digital decluttering can help you manage this overwhelming feeling, reduce stress, and live a happier life with more time to discover your meaning and purpose.

In addition, a cluttered digital workspace accumulates a lot of data and information that negatively impacts both your devices and your behavior.

For example, a cluttered desktop makes it irritating to search through countless files for official documents; hence the importance of digital decluttering.

In this part of the book, we will talk about how to get started.

If you are new to digital decluttering, you may feel puzzled, confused, and overwhelmed.

Don't worry. We will answer all your questions in this book, and this section is focused on helping you get started on this journey to freedom.

How to use this book

One Click Away is divided into several parts, each with different chapters that will guide you on how to declutter digitally, how to practice it, and how to stick with it for the long haul.

This book is designed to add convenience to your life. It is not your regular A-Z book where you have to start at chapter one and systematically go through the chapters one by one in order to understand or use the content in the book.

With this book, you can read and learn at your convenience. You can start from the very first part of the book or even from the last part.

You can read all the chapters in any part, skim through the chapters, or read just any chapter you like. Even in the middle of a chapter, you can pick out the part that resonates with you the most and read it.

Let's begin this journey that will help you shift and pivot your way to a decluttered, organized, and peaceful life, both in your heart and in your mind.

There is no need to feel overwhelmed. If you do, it's because you have too much in front of you and don't know what to do with it. Our goal is to take things from complexity to simplicity.

As you read through this book, I want you to remember this:

"Simplicity is the key to mastery, and complexity is the path to chaos."

My goal with *One Click Away* is to lead you away from the complexity of the chaos that has become your digital hell and into an easy-to-manage system.

Now that you're ready, let's turn the page and get started...

Part 1: Warning Signs of Digital Declutter and the Digital Declutter Method

Chapter 1: Getting Started with the Basics

To achieve any goal, you must start with the basics. That is why we will dive into the specifics, help you understand digital hoarding, and then move on to decluttering.

What is digital hoarding?

"Digital hoarding is the accumulation of digital files to the point of loss of perspective, which ultimately leads to stress and disorganization.

The reluctance to get rid of digital data you no longer value leads to digital hoarding, e-clutter, e-hoarding, cyber hoarding, and data hoarding.

Digital hoarding occurs in electronic environments because it involves storing information digitally.

The term digital hoarding gained worldwide acceptance after the study conducted by Van Bennekom and his collaborators in 2015. Also, did you know that there is a close relationship between individuals with physical and digital hoarding behaviors?

So, *how can you tell if you are a digital hoarder?*

Anyone can be a victim of having cluttered data on their device and/or inbox. At the same time, they may deny that they have such useless data, photos, unread emails, unused apps, and similar data.

Digital hoarding has become a global problem due to the availability of faster Internet, high-tech devices, and various types of storage.

Now that we have unlimited space to store data that we may use later, we continue to store more data, adding to the clutter and worsening our mental health due to the level of multitasking triggered by trying to manage all the information.

You are a digital hoarder if you have any of the following:

- A collection of used or broken devices

- A desktop cluttered with icons and folders

- Duplicate files on a device and cloud services

- Over 20 bookmarks - possibly hundreds

- Apps you've never used and don't even know what they are

- Social media accounts with friends you don't know and multiple photo books

- Problems finding things because of clutter

- Expanded digital space that takes more time and adds to the clutter

Let's take a look at the different types of digital hoarders to make sure you know what kind of hoarder you are.

Types of Digital Hoarders

There are four types of digital hoarders:

1. **The collector**

2. **The accidental hoarder**

3. **The fearful hoarder**

4. **The Compliant Hoarder**

1: The Compliant Hoarder

Some organizations require their employees to keep data longer because they need to use it for future reference.

People who hoard out of compliance with their organization are called "compliant hoarders" or "hoarders by instruction. This type of hoarding is often associated with the workplace.

Many companies have correspondence systems that use email for decision-making and official approvals. Therefore, employees need to keep these emails for later review and security.

Therefore, compliant hoarders are not emotionally attached to the digital clutter and are more likely to delete it when the data is no longer needed.

2: The accidental or disengaged hoarder

The term accidental hoarder refers to the disorganized hoarder who is unaware of the data they have kept for a long time.

Accidental hoarders don't realize they've been keeping data for a while, but they still have data randomly stored on their digital devices.

As the name implies, you are a hoarder by accident, not by choice. You don't have a specific method of hoarding, and your primary characteristics are laziness or lack of interest in organizing data properly, which is how data accumulates over time.

The lack of active management habits leads you, the disengaged hoarder, to accidentally end up with a digital mess.

3: The Collector

The collector is the organized hoarder who keeps track of all the data he or she collects. This type of hoarder is organized, systematic, and in control of all their data-and it's usually a lot.

The collector is likely to have systemized all the digital clutter and divided it into different categories.

For example, there may be separate folders for different documents, audio files, and videos. The collector has properly labeled and organized the stored data.

Despite the collector's efforts to store data neatly, there is a lot of data, and most of it is usually redundant. There may be old files that the collector hasn't used in ages. For example, there may be photos from a wedding 10 years ago that no one, not even the collector, looks at.

If you have dozens of properly labeled folders and tons of very neatly categorized data that you have not touched in years, you know you are in this category.

4: The anxious hoarder

The anxious hoarder is the one who has developed an emotional attachment to the data they collect.

This digital hoarder is afraid to get rid of any data because they feel it might be needed at some point or in the future. The anxious hoarder keeps the data on the premise that he may need it in an emergency.

To some extent, the accumulation of old data becomes a source of comfort and security for the hoarder. This hoarder sees all the clutter as useful for the future, not realizing that it is negatively affecting them.

If you are an anxious hoarder, it is likely that you are constantly hoarding all kinds of digital data on the premise that it will come in handy in the future.

Now that you know the types of hoarders, it is easy to study them and find out which type you are.

Here's what you need to do.

1. Find out your type of hoarder

2. Study each type for 5 minutes.

3. Compare your behavior to each type.

4. Once you understand your type, you can observe the appropriate behaviors.

5. Once you know your digital hoarder type, you can move on, which starts with becoming fully aware of the harms of digital hoarding.

In the next chapter, we'll discuss the overwhelming nature of hoarding and the consequences of digital clutter.

Chapter 2: The Consequences of Digital Clutter

Sometimes it can be difficult to see how digital clutter is overwhelming us, which may explain why we continue to fall into the digital hoarding trap.

This chapter looks at the consequences of digital clutter to motivate you to do something about it.

Digital clutter causes stress

Did you know that digital hoarding and clutter can cause stress?

A survey of more than 2,000 consumers found that increased digital clutter during the COVID-19 shutdown increased stress levels.

When you have lots of emails to respond to, newsletters to read, data to choose from, files to select from, and pictures to flip through, it can be overwhelming.

And, when you have a lot of data, especially unorganized data, finding the right file or piece of information at the right time can be an uphill battle. All of this adds to your stress.

Increases cyber risks

According to a Kaspersky Lab study, "Sorting out digital clutter in business," there is a correlation between digital clutter and cybersecurity.

The report found that when we have a lot of digital clutter, we often forget to back up important documents that contain sensitive and personally identifiable information that could potentially harm us or our business because we have so much information and data at our disposal.

Another study found that digital clutter often encourages users to be careless, exposing their digital devices and sensitive information to security threats and vulnerabilities.

Slowing down devices

This survey shows that of all the applications we install on our computers, we never use 30% of them, which means we are constantly adding software and applications to our digital devices that we do not necessarily use. This clutter slows down our devices.

Digital hoarding wastes limited time

Say you need to email an important file to a client, but you can't find it in all the clutter on your hard drive.

You want to find the link to a job application site you bookmarked, but you can't find it among the thousands of other bookmarks.

You have a webinar to attend, but you cannot find the email with the link to the webinar invitation because your inbox is overflowing with new, unread emails.

Time is money, but you keep wasting it because of all the digital clutter in your life. This is a big reason why you never get anything done on time and are behind on most of your tasks. How do you fix the problem? Get rid of what you don't need and haven't used in months or years.

Increases mental fatigue

When you can't get things done on time, have too much on your plate, struggle with FOMO (fear of missing out), and have too much on your plate, you naturally experience mental fatigue.

According to psychologist Donna Ferguson, Ph.D., clutter of any kind, including digital clutter, leads to mental fatigue and tension.

Digital clutter takes up space on your digital devices and in your mind. Staying glued to screens, struggling to find things among thousands of pieces of data, missing important tasks, missing deadlines, and other problems caused by digital clutter take a toll on your mental well-being.

Leads to procrastination

Clutter and procrastination are closely related. Finding the right files or data can be difficult when you have more digital data to manage. So instead of sifting through all the data and information to find what you are looking for, you procrastinate.

You may also get sidetracked from the task you were working on because something else caught your attention while you were trying to do something, and before you know it, you are no longer doing what you were originally doing.

There are other drawbacks and negative effects of digital hoarding and clutter.

Other negative consequences of digital overload

- Using your phone before bed keeps your brain active and it becomes a struggle to fall asleep.

- You become addicted to the online world and want to do all activities online, such as playing, shopping, selling, earning, reading, etc.

- You stay online unnecessarily all the time, scrolling down the newsfeed and becoming mentally saturated. You may not realize it now, but this pressure to be everywhere is affecting your mental well-being.

- You keep accumulating data without realizing its irrelevance. You struggle to delete old stuff and think more than you need to before you get rid of even a photo from the Internet.

- You may find yourself running from one task to another, trying to do everything in a frenzy and often not getting anything done.

- If you often feel irritable and tired every time you step away from the digital world, it is a sign that you are digitally overwhelmed. It can lead to headaches and abrupt behavior.

- You struggle with *Fear of Missing Out* (FOMO) and find yourself staring at your screen, scrolling through your news feed, looking at tweet after tweet, constantly hoarding data just to make sure you don't miss an important find? If so, you have a big problem.

- You have over 100 unopened chats on your phone.

- If you have hundreds or thousands of unopened emails and your email inbox is filling up, you're clearly holding on to data you don't need.

- If you keep buying USBs, drives, and storage devices just to store more data you never use, you are a data hoarder and need help.

When you use the Internet, you open multiple tabs at the same time. Even when you're done with a tab, you don't close it right away; you leave it hanging for a long time.

If any of this sounds familiar, you need help getting rid of your digital clutter.

Hey, don't worry. We're here to simplify your life, and the next part of the book is focused on helping you get started on your digital decluttering journey.

For now, since you've analyzed the downsides of digital clutter, let me walk you through what happens when you practice digital decluttering.

Chapter 3: The Benefits of Digital Decluttering

Decluttering your physical and digital spaces is a highly effective way to make your life more productive and satisfying.

Let me boost your motivation to do what's necessary by highlighting all the different ways digital decluttering improves your life, so that by the time you finish this chapter, you'll feel ready to take the plunge.

Speed up your computer

You probably feel frustrated when your computer is slow. But did you know that it is slow because of all the redundant data and information you have stored on it?

The more data your computer stores, the harder its processor works. Plus, lots of applications and software running in the background can slow your system down, draining processing power and battery life.

The solution to a sluggish computer is in your hands: declutter!

Removing unnecessary files, documents, and pictures that you no longer need, or use can take anywhere from minutes to hours (or more), depending on the size of the file. However, this effort will greatly improve the speed of your device.

Dramatically increase productivity

When you have so many emails, you have to scroll through several read and unread emails to get to the one you want.

This scrolling means you waste important time that could be spent doing something productive. Sometimes you even forget why you opened your Gmail account, and you can easily find yourself using social media apps because you feel bored.

These problems are easy to deal with once you start decluttering your digital life. You'll be able to find what you're looking for with ease, and you'll notice a remarkable increase in productivity.

Gives you a fresh start

Getting rid of your digital clutter makes room for new projects and gives you more space to work and mental freedom. It provides a fresh start for storing updated and enhanced information and tools.

After removing old and outdated files, you will notice updated tools and versions on your desktop.

Improves your focus

Digital decluttering also improves your ability to focus. When you do not have information, data, and files that can easily steal your concentration and attention, you can focus on more important things that you need to work on at any given time.

From having an organized email, to having all your files in one place, to having a dedicated folder for all your pictures, to not having extra documents, when things are streamlined and clutter-free, you become more focused and dedicated to your work!

Reduces stress and anxiety

How does it feel to have to turn on your laptop or go through your phone when you have countless files, documents, apps, software, thousands of pictures, etc.? Overwhelming, right?

Now imagine switching between devices and navigating with ease because you're organized. Doesn't that feel better?

When you get rid of all the unnecessary stuff, you begin to restore order to your life because you only have what you need, and that feels so good.

Reduces the risk of Shiny Object Syndrome

Shiny Object Syndrome (SOS) is a disorder in which you get distracted or seduced by any other thing that seems attractive and pleasant. It makes you focus on everything new and trendy, changing your course and track.

Digital overload increases the risk of SOS. When you spend unnecessary time on different social platforms, you see a lot of advertisements that make you buy new services or products. It is also easy to get distracted from your goals by wasting energy on the wrong things.

Digital decluttering limits what you expose yourself to, eliminating unnecessary digital clutter. It makes you more focused, which helps you avoid shiny object syndrome.

It makes it easier to start tasks

Just as a messy room or desk can be annoying and uncomfortable, so too can a cluttered desktop.

Once you start decluttering and deleting unused files or unnecessary documents, the bombardment of information and data stops, making it relatively easy to start and complete your tasks.

And, because decluttering improves your attention span, you can focus more on specific tasks.

Part 2: The Digital Declutter Method

The 11 Step Method to Reclaiming Your Productivity

Digital clutter refers to all the unnecessary applications, extensions, files, folders, and other digital data on your desktop, phone, or laptop.

So far, you have a pretty good idea of digital clutter and how it is overwhelming you. Now let me introduce you to the solution to your problem: digital decluttering.

This part of the book will help you understand the digital decluttering method, how to get started, and an easy 11-step method you can use to perform digital decluttering to reclaim your productivity.

Decluttering can feel overwhelming if you've become accustomed to storing too much data and information on your phone, tablet, or laptop. Going through it all to delete and organize what you don't use can feel wasteful - like you're undoing a lot of work.

The best way to do this is to set aside 30 minutes a day to declutter.

It is also best to do one thing at a time. For example, if you start decluttering your email, focus on that specific task until it is finished. Once it is done, you can move on to something else, such as decluttering your desktop, files, email, and all the spaces in between that need to be cleaned up.

Chapter 4: The Basics of Digital Declutter

Digital decluttering means removing unnecessary and useless digital clutter from your life.

One digital clutter survey found that the average person has:

- 183 bookmarks

- 27 tabs open in their browser

- 15+ unread emails

- 20 desktop icons

- 13 unused phone applications

- 582 saved phone pictures

- 2 broken or unused phones

- 209 GB of cloud storage

- 4 external hard drives

- 654 GB of external storage

The statistics show that we are all hoarders in one way or another, and we need to step up our decluttering game.

The cold turkey approach never works in the long run because you are likely to have a rebound period and revert to your digital hoarding ways.

It is best to take the slow and steady approach. Here's what you need to do:

Assess where you are

The first step to a streamlined digital life is to identify where you are right now. This means assessing your level of digital decluttering.

Clutter creates stress, so you need to assess the factors that are creating clutter in your digital workspace.

Before you jump into organizing your digital home, here's how you can assess if you need to declutter your digital workspace without procrastinating:

Take an inventory of your folders and applications to analyze the last time you used them.

Check how much space you have left on your device. Most of the time, you don't have enough space to download important documents because of the huge amount of space taken up by junk.

See if it is annoying to get the needed file or mail while browsing through thousands of spam and accumulated junk.

See if the speed of your device is slow or if it's annoying to waste time waiting to open a file.

Once you have completed this assessment, you should focus on how to clean up the entire digital clutter.

Once you have completed this step, take an inventory of your emotions and see how you are feeling. If you feel overwhelmed, take a few deep breaths, take a break, drink something refreshing, and then move on to the next step.

Create a list of your digital spaces in categories

When it comes to storing our digital media, many of us have a "save it or lose it" mentality.

We feel the need to save every file, image, document, audio, etc. that we receive - just in case we might need it someday. That's how many of us end up hoarding digital clutter. Understand that hoarding only increases your stress level.

After assessing your condition, you need to start decluttering by categorizing your digital spaces.

Let's look at our digital universe and determine what contributes to our digital hoarding.

Here is how to inventory or categorize what you need to declutter in your digital space:

#1: Computer Desktop:

The following digital possessions that inhabit your computer desktop are in dire need of disposal:

- Applications

- Browsers

- Cloud-based storage

- Desktop folders

- Download Folders

- Files and documents

- Passwords and logins

- Photos and screenshots

#2: Work applications:

Cluttered work applications can include:

- Emails

- Google Drive

- Inbox

- Miscellaneous documents

- Notes

- Passwords and logins

- Project Management Tools

- Reminders

- Slack channels and messages

#3: Mobile or tablet:

The messiest nest of clutter in your digital space is the phone or tablet you keep by your side most, if not all, of the time.

The following areas deserve your priority as you clean up your device:

- Apps

- Emails

- Home screens

- Music libraries

- Notes app

- Notifications

- Phone contacts

- Photos and screenshots

- Voicemails and texts

Once you have created all these categories, you need to audit them individually to see how much clutter you have in each category.

Auditing Your Digital Universe

Auditing the digital universe means examining the digital space to sort out the clutter created by digital hoarding on your devices.

It is about analyzing your use and benefit of stored content so that you have a clear idea of how and where to begin digital decluttering.

Simply put, auditing the digital universe is like looking at a road map before starting a journey to reach a destination.

Now that you have all the categories in place, here's what you need to do:

- Scrutinize all files and folders to set aside the data you think is worth keeping, and may prove useful in the future.
- Delete all files, images, audio, documents, etc. that you no longer need.
- Anything older than six months that has served its purpose should be thrown in the trash.
- See if you are holding on to anything that is useless on a personal level. You may have pictures that your friend asked you to save. Since they serve no purpose, it is okay to throw them away.

After auditing your digital universe, you must begin the 11-step decluttering process.

The following chapters will teach you how to do this.

Chapter 5: Cleaning Out Email Clutter

Dealing with email can be especially challenging because your email account may have a lot of unwanted emails.

With so many newsletters and emails coming into your inbox, you may miss important emails. That's why it's important to clean up your email inbox and folders.

You can follow the steps below to get rid of email clutter.

Step 1: Clean up your email inbox

Every time you open your email, you see lots of unread emails from companies advertising products and services. You hardly ever read any of them.

It's better to clean out your email inbox by deleting all the emails, or you can archive all the messages.

If you have a huge inbox, your best bet is to declare email inbox bankruptcy. This means that you archive your messages to ensure that you do not have to see a full inbox. To do this, check the "select all" box, then click "select all (number of emails)" conversations in the inbox, and then click the down arrow to archive all conversations.

If you don't want to archive messages, you can create labels in Gmail to receive specific emails in specific folders/labels. For example, I've created different labels like work, education, finance, etc. So try these features to see if it works for you.

Step 2: Unsubscribe 99% of the time

You don't unsubscribe from email newsletters because you think you might need them later! But you literally don't.

If you don't want to receive these emails, you need to unsubscribe from these products, campaigns, and organizations.

There are two ways to do this:

You can **manually unsubscribe** from emails; or,

Use an email unsubscribe service. There is an unsubscribe option at the bottom of every email, but if you want to continue receiving email from a particular site or company, you can set email preferences to receive fewer updates. Typically, most emails have a link at the bottom to set your preferences (some only have an unsubscribe option).

Create criteria for unsubscribing. For example, unsubscribe from emails you never read, companies that send too many promotional emails, or other irrelevant emails in your inbox.

Step 3: Unsubscribe from newsletters

Not every newsletter is important or helpful to you. If you have subscribed to dozens of newsletters, you will notice that your Gmail inbox is always full of unread emails. A full inbox can make it overwhelming to find important emails.

Unsubscribe from all irrelevant newsletters. Although Gmail has a separate section for promotional newsletters, you need to unsubscribe from them to streamline your inbox. For example, you can unsubscribe from online shopping deal newsletters.

Set personal priorities or criteria and unsubscribe from all irrelevant newsletters. To unsubscribe from newsletters, you can follow the same steps: open the newsletter, scroll to the bottom (some have an unsubscribe option at the top), and unsubscribe or set preferences.

Some other steps you can take to stay focused while you work are

Don't always keep the email tab open in your browser.

Instead, check your email periodically, perhaps once or twice a day. This will help you focus on your other tasks. Instead of keeping the email tab open 24/7 and checking it all the time, set aside time to check your email. This strategy allows you to focus on your work and ensures that random emails do not distract you.

Set filters to automatically file various emails in a specific folder, skip the inbox, or never reach spam. Use these filters to time-block and task-batch your email use. For example, if you need to review all emails related to new career opportunities during a specific time window, filter the job notification emails to skip your inbox and go directly to a specific folder. You can then check that particular folder at a specific time of day.

Become someone who responds to email appropriately, not quickly. Not every email is necessary, and not every email requires your immediate response. Remember that the more email you read, the more email you get. Ignore all emails that do not require a response. Gradually build your reputation as someone who takes the time to respond to the right emails, not just every email.

If you want more focus, fewer distractions, and more time for important tasks, clean up and organize your inbox according to your personal preferences.

PRO TIP: For the next two weeks, open every email and newsletter, unsubscribe, or adjust your email preferences to suit your needs.

Don't procrastinate - take action now towards your email clutter to achieve a more balanced digital life.

Chapter 6: Clean Up Your Laptop and Bookmarks

Your computer probably needs a lot of tidying up. If you have files and documents scattered all over your desktop, you feel a sense of chaos every time you start working on your device.

Don't worry, we've got you covered. We'll walk you through cleaning up your laptop and bookmarks so you don't feel so exhausted.

Step 4: Delete and Organize Laptop Icons and Folders

Our laptop/desktop often acts as a dumping ground for our random files and folders.

Anything that does not have a permanent home, such as downloads, shortcuts, pictures, notes, installers, and other digital detritus, acts as a distraction on your laptop. This mass of folders and icons gets in the way of a smooth computing experience.

You can follow these steps to clean up and organize folders and icons. You can start by cleaning up your desktop.

To give your desktop a clean and uncluttered look:

Organize it into folders and subfolders.

Take a look at your desktop and see if the items you drop on your desktop fall into some categories, such as downloads, application shortcuts, and work documents.

Create folders and subfolders and drop the files into the appropriate folders and subfolders. This will significantly reduce the number of icons and folders on your desktop.

Delete all irrelevant files and items you don't need anymore.

If you are using Windows and want to create a folder, right-click on an empty part of the desktop and select 'New', then select the folder. On MacOS, ctrl-click and select 'New Folder'.

Step 5: Delete bookmarks and organize them into folders

Do you often bookmark sites for future reference? Let me know how often you refer to these bookmarks. Never or rarely, right?

Too many bookmarks just take up space on your computer and in your mind. When you open a bookmark, you get distracted and go to another site that you never intended to visit. So the more bookmarks you have, the more clutter in your life. Now is the best time to get rid of them, too.

Set a bookmark limit of between 5 and 20 bookmarks. Delete the ones you can and store the others in apps like Evernote or Pocket. Then monitor yourself monthly to see which of these bookmarks you are using.

Make sure you do not succumb to the urge to create more bookmarks in the future. Instead, close a site after you use it. If you feel like bookmarking a site, consider whether you will use it.

If you bookmark it, that's okay. Revisit all of your newly added bookmarks every five days. If you haven't visited those sites in the last five days, delete them. This way, you'll slowly break the habit and eliminate excessive bookmarking.

Step 6: Get rid of old data and documents

Did you know that most people have a "just in case" syndrome where they hold on to their old data and documents and never delete them?

"Let's keep this picture in case it comes in handy for a report."

"Let's keep this song in case I need to listen to it while traveling."

"Let's keep these movies for days when I have sleepovers with friends."

"Let's not delete my college thesis in case I need it for work."

These or similar examples may resonate with you.

When we have the "just in case" syndrome, we are likely to hold on to things because we think they might be useful.

To increase your productivity, you need to address this syndrome, and yes, it starts with deleting all the extra documents and data.

No matter how important you think a document is, if it has been sitting aimlessly on your digital devices for months, it is time to throw it in the digital trash.

Here are the steps to take:

First, sort your records by date and start deleting duplicate files.

If you really need some data for later use, create a folder for it and delete other data you no longer need.

Now, let's move on to the next step and bring more structure to your life.

Chapter 7: Moving Data to the Cloud

If your computer is running low on storage, it might be due to unnecessary saved data clogging your system.

Do you have a lot of pictures, videos, and other files that you don't want to delete?

Those items take up too much space on your laptop, slowing it down. You can try storing them externally. One example of such external storage is the cloud storage system.

You can move your data to cloud drives as these are the best place to store your pictures, videos, and other documents.

Step 7: Familiarize Yourself with Cloud Usage

We often miss out on many helpful and unique tools because we don't understand them. One example is cloud storage.

If you are using Windows or Mac, they give you options of storing your data outside your computer storage and from where you can download and use them anytime.

Many cloud storage solutions like Google Drive, iCloud, Dropbox, etc., are available for your usage pleasure. Not familiarizing yourself with these systems keeps you from leveraging them properly.

For example, when users set auto backups and syncs, it results in hogging a lot of storage. You need to figure out one or two cloud storage solutions you would like to work with and start using them regularly to streamline your digital universe.

Here is how you can do this:

- Start acclimating yourself to these cloud systems.

- Dedicate some time, say 20 minutes every month, to understanding how and where you back up your files.
- Understand its settings and adjust them according to your requirements to get the most out of them.
- As you become more knowledgeable about using a cloud system, select the data you wish to keep on your digital devices.
- Transfer data from devices to the cloud. This may take some time, so feel free to tend to other tasks while the data is uploading.
- Work on uploading your data in this manner for a couple of days until you have all your important data and files transferred to the cloud.

As you start using the cloud more, you will notice a new sense of peace entering your life. You won't worry much about the storage devices swarming with data. Neither will you have to delete files from them time and again.

However, if you keep hoarding data on the cloud, there may come a time when it may fill up with clutter. To keep that infamous day from approaching, declutter your cloud spaces.

Step 8: Declutter Your Digital Storage Spaces (Cloud Space, Data Storage Apps)

Virtual/digital storage spaces like iCloud help you control your computer clutter, but it will add stress and frustration if this digital storage gets cluttered, too.

If you save everything on your virtual storage spaces, they will also become full, and you will have to buy more storage.

Ensure this does not happen by developing the habit of cleaning these storage spaces.

Implement these steps:

1. Delete anything you don't need and adjust settings accordingly.

2. Scan the cloud and delete any file, image, audio, video, image, or other data you have used. If you wish to keep anything, make a folder and save it.

3. Organize everything into folders and subfolders and set aside some time to declutter this digital storage space.

We tend to develop a strong affiliation with our pictures and the many memories they hold for us. While that is understandable, this bond often makes us hoard pictures, resulting in digital piles of clutter.

It is possible that when you have the option of saving things on the cloud, you start storing more data on it to save more memories.

Make sure to take stock of your emotions from time to time so that if you find yourself harboring such feelings, you can manage them and gently work on them.

To manage your feelings about pictures, tune into the respective memory associated with a photo. For instance, if you are looking at a picture of yourself posing with your child, see if that particular picture genuinely matters to you. Is it from the day something special happened? If you can vaguely recall the day, chances are it is just your brain playing games with you, trying to make you hold on to the clutter.

Take a deep breath and try to calm yourself. Tell yourself that this memory is nothing more than a photo, and that deleting it won't affect you in any significant way.

Next, motivate yourself to delete it. Use this approach to delete more of your pictures, images, and other data for which you may have developed strong emotions or associations.

Use this approach to declutter the cloud on a regular basis.

Declutter your streaming services and music files.

Music is food for the soul. But all that music on your laptop, phone, and streaming services is cluttering up your digital world.

Store and back up all your music: Just like your photos and documents, save and back up all your music files. Delete them all from your laptop, tablet, phone, and other digital devices and streaming services and upload them to the cloud. If you have a large music library, consider an external hard drive.

Have a folder system: Have a folder called "music" and use it to organize all your music files. A good folder structure is music > artist > release date > audio/artwork files. You can also have a 'different artists' subfolder for different compilations.

Put all the music into the new folders: Next, file all the music into the new folders. Be sure to delete any duplicate tracks. Also, if you no longer listen to certain podcasts, audio files, and songs, delete them instead of keeping them for a time when you might want to listen to them again. If that time has not yet come, it is highly unlikely that it will.

Rename the unnamed music files: Now is the time to rename the "unknown tracks" so that you can easily find them when you need to. You can listen to them manually and rename them or use an application like 'MusicBrainz Picard' that automatically recognizes music metadata.

Organize music from streaming services into playlists: If you use a music streaming app like Spotify or SoundCloud, organize all your songs there into different playlists by artist, genre, mood, etc. The more organized your playlist is, the less clutter you will have and the more time you will save.

Once you have completed this step, it is time to **focus on social media**.

Scott Allan

Chapter 8:
Managing Social
Media Content

Social media has become an integral part of our lives. While Facebook, Instagram, Twitter, TikTok, Pinterest, LinkedIn and various other social media sites allow us to connect, their overuse can distract us, causing anxiety and frustration.

First, let's look at why you need to unplug from social media and go on a social media detox.

Why do a social media detox?

While the lives of those on social media seem pretty "shiny and perfect," understand that everyone, yes, EVERYONE, is going through a personal struggle. What seems true on social media isn't always true. So, you may be

56

following someone who appears to be living the "perfect life," but deep down they are struggling with unseen demons.

When we follow social media ideals, we fall prey to false ideologies and begin to think the same way.

Somehow, we aspire to live their lives. Driven by this ambition, we disregard our own blessings.

This is one of the ways in which social media distracts us from a contented and happy life and creates tension.

The more you engage in social media, the more it clutters your life and your mind. You may spend hours taking the perfect selfies and then even more time posting them online, applying the most appropriate filters, and then waiting for the post to get maximum likes and reactions.

Driven by the desire to create the most engaging posts, you may accumulate many images, audio files, videos, and other data on your phone, tablet, and laptop.

You may also find yourself downloading every new app that's trending, or even those that aren't.

Soon you will feel the need to be the star of every social media platform, whether it is TikTok, Snapchat, Twitter, or any other platform. If it is out there, you have to be on it.

This is how social media wraps you in its vicious wings and takes you over. This change may not be permanent, but it lasts a long time and consumes your well-being.

The digital clutter in your digital devices and the mental clutter in your mind, courtesy of social media, is quite devastating.

Since you want to be happy and live a thriving life, it is important to breathe some freedom into your life. This "breath of fresh air" can only come from decluttering your social media life.

Mind you, I'm not saying you shouldn't use social media. I'm saying you don't have to abuse it, or let social media abuse you!

Let's discuss some simple steps you can take to declutter your social media life.

Step 9: Set Intentions to Engage in a Social Media Purge

Most studies show that people who spend more time on social media without a clear purpose have low self-esteem, feel lonely, and are more anxious and depressed.

Not everything on social media is for you. You're not missing anything by not using social media.

You need to understand and remember this in order to set a firm intention to clean up your social media accounts. After all, the journey to any goal begins with an unwavering intention.

Therefore, the journey to a social media purge must begin with a clear intention to get off social media and cleanse your accounts of unnecessary stuff.

Here's what you need to do:

- Think about all the ways social media is weighing you down.

- Write them down.

- Next, think about how a social media purge will bring sanity to your life and make you feel better.

- Explore these reasons and visualize yourself living a peaceful life without social media clutter.

- Now create the intention to indulge in the cleansing.

- Say the intention out loud first, then write it down. The intention can be something like, "I am engaging in a social media purge to bring clarity and peace to my life.

- Next, go through all of your social media accounts, one at a time, and examine them in detail.

- Delete all unused, irrelevant, and old files, pictures, accounts, etc. from your social media accounts.

The best way to do this is to go slow, rather than attacking all accounts like a Spartan warrior. For example, spend a week cleaning up Snapchat, then tackle Facebook the next week. You can then work on Instagram the week after that and Twitter the week after that.

Use this step-by-step approach to stick with your cleanup and get your social media accounts in order.

Step 10: Disconnect from social media accounts

Disengagement from social media is very important. You can't do a complete social cleanse without disengaging from the social media world for a while.

However, this does not mean that you should stop using social media altogether. It just means that you need to limit your interaction with the platforms.

Here are some things you should do to disengage from social media platforms:

Set a time limit on social media use. For example, set aside 30 minutes twice a day to use social media. If this is too little time compared to the many hours you currently spend on the platforms, you can spend two hours. However, you need to reduce the time.

Make sure you only use social media during the time you set aside.

Set reminders on your phone and write reminders on your fridge, bedroom wall, etc. to make sure you stick to the habit.

Create a social media-free corner in your home, and when you are in that space, do not use social media at all, not even a filtered photo.

When you do use social media, unfollow or unfriend the pages and people that you don't engage with or that are irrelevant to you. This will help you find relevant things without scrolling through your news feed. If you follow an account that makes you feel inadequate or lacking - because of the luxury life it shows - unfollow it.

Log out of your social media accounts so that every time you need to log in, you have to manually enter your username and password. Since this takes time, it automatically reduces your urge to use the platforms.

As you work through these guidelines, you will gradually reduce your addiction to social media.

Step 11: Purge weekly, monthly, or quarterly

You will start to feel good about yourself when you clean up your social media. Make a routine of cleaning up this digital mess according to your availability so you don't feel overwhelmed.

It is in your best interest to establish a weekly, monthly, or quarterly routine to clean up your chaotic digital mess. This step will give you peace of mind and make your digital life simpler and more balanced.

Here's how you can get started on a weekly, monthly, and then quarterly cleanup:

Start by not using social media for a few hours.

Once you get used to not using social media for 6 to 12 hours for a couple of weeks, try not using it for a full day.

If you can go 24 hours without touching any social media platform on any digital device, go another 24 hours with a one-day break.

After a week, increase this period to 2 to 3 days.

Next, up the ante by going on a crazy week-long cleanse and see if you can pull it off. During this time, stock up on your favorite music and reading material, and do other fun things you've been meaning to do, such as painting, biking, picnicking, etc.

Once you have successfully completed a one-week social media detox, practice it at least once a month.

After a couple of months of this, go on a month-long purge.

Once you get the hang of it, make it a quarterly thing and you'll find yourself in better control of your social media use.

Now all you need to do is build on this momentum and continue to declutter your life digitally.

One of the most important keys to sticking with this practice is to build a lifestyle around it.

You need to develop the urge to live a digitally minimalist life; that's how you'll gradually rid yourself of all the unnecessary clutter.

The next part of the book will teach you how to do this.

Part 3: Creating Digital Minimalism

Minimalism has many definitions, and people perceive it differently.

Some see it as a way to consume less, while others see it as a way of life that allows them to focus on what brings them joy.

The concept is also approached differently in different cultures and takes on different forms when applied to different areas of life.

In your digital life, minimalism is about wanting less, sticking to what matters most, and breathing ease, peace, and grace into your life.

Earlier we talked about our tendency to associate certain images with certain memories.

Many of us do the same with many other things in our lives: clothes, toys, ornaments, books, and yes, digital devices and data.

We tend to stock up on broken and used digital devices and fail to throw them away for a variety of reasons.

Data remains in our devices as long as we are willing to tolerate it. We keep adding more data to our lives, even though we have yet to use the data we have already accumulated.

The same goes for digital devices. We keep buying more without making good use of the ones we already have.

The previous parts of the book have described such behaviors and their negative effects. Therefore, we will not go into those details again. However, we will relate them to the need to apply minimalism in our lives.

Chapter 9: How Digital Minimalism Declutters Your Digital Universe

Why do we feel the need to hoard?

One of the main factors that contributes to our desire to hoard things, including digital devices, data, and tools, is our inability to distinguish between our real needs and those we absorb from our environment.

Maybe you saw an ad for an iPad and immediately felt the urge to buy one. Maybe you saw all your friends playing a social media game and wanted to join in.

Suppose we continue to absorb all these emotions and unnecessary needs from our environment. In this case, we will continue to respond to these urges, and by responding to them, we will increase our digital clutter.

In addition, our laziness, just-in-case syndrome, shiny object syndrome, and other issues discussed earlier in the book cause us to hoard in one way or another.

Unfortunately, we have become so accustomed to adding clutter to our lives that we don't see it as a problem until it takes a massive toll on our mental health and quality of life.

Even when we try to practice digital decluttering, we find ourselves returning to the same old routine after a while because we haven't addressed the root cause.

We remove some clutter from the surface, but we never really get to the bottom of it. As a result, many of our clutter-related problems persist.

Digital minimalism offers you an escape from all this. We will also discuss how you can use digital minimalism to further streamline your life to avoid relapsing into digital hoarding, remove all the clutter where it accumulates the most, and best manage your digital life.

Digital minimalism is a way of life: a lifestyle of peace, clarity, and freedom.

Here's how digital minimalism gives you that freedom of choice and clarity:

It helps you clarify your needs.

Minimalism is about knowing what you want and being clear about it.

You take into account your true wants and needs, and you learn to separate them from the superficial desires you absorb from your environment.

Once you can do this, you can better identify what you need and what you want.

With this sense of awareness, you find yourself stepping away from digital clutter easily and slowly discarding all the digital clutter you have hoarded over the years.

Allows you to learn how to keep what brings you joy

Digital minimalism is never about frugality or not wanting high-tech gadgets or the latest software and apps. I know tech-savvy digital minimalists who have the latest iPhone and accessories.

But I know you won't find unnecessary gadgets in this friend's home. This friend uses his phone alone for almost everything: creating documents, taking photos, sending emails, and editing images, among many other technological tasks.

Digital minimalism is about sticking to digital technologies and data that add value to your life.

So, if a high-end laptop adds convenience to your life, keep it, but get rid of the other devices you have kept for no reason.

Similarly, keep the data, bookmarks, pictures, and apps you really need, and get rid of everything else. That's how you declutter your digital universe and stick to what really makes you happy.

Focus on what matters

We tend to get distracted because we are surrounded by myriad distractions. Too many apps, too many tools, and too much data can distract even the best of us.

When you apply minimalism to your digital universe, you stay with the things that really matter to you. As a result, your sense of focus improves and your energy shifts to the important things in life.

Avoid Hoarding Relapse

Just as addicts experience relapse, you can experience hoarding relapse even after a good period of decluttering. The main characteristic of such a relapse is the need to re-hoard digital stuff, including devices, tools, software, applications, data, information, etc.

The main reason you fall prey to a hoarding relapse is that you may still harbor unnecessary emotions and superficial desires for digital hoarding.

While you may believe that hoarding is unhealthy on the surface, it's only a superficial change. It is very likely that somewhere deep down you still believe that you need more digital devices and that the more digital tools you have, the better.

When you religiously follow digital minimalism, you gradually rid yourself of false and meaningless desires and understand what you really want and what gives you meaning. As a result, you eliminate the unnecessary desires that give rise to digital hoarding.

When you eliminate the root cause, the likelihood of relapse is automatically reduced to the bare minimum. This is exactly how digital minimalism helps you avoid digital hoarding relapse.

Makes you eliminate the useless

A digital minimalist lifestyle makes you prioritize yourself and your real needs. You gain self-awareness that encourages you to make healthy and informed choices, allowing you to eliminate all the useless stuff from your life.

As a result, all sorts of digital clutter gradually disappear from your life, leaving more room for less, and less is more.

Now you understand how digital minimalism can make your life easier. Let's discuss three steps to wanting less and focusing on what matters to you.

Chapter 10: How to Want Less in Life

The journey to a peaceful life begins with wanting less. I know this can be a bit of a struggle, especially since we live in a consumer society that encourages wanting and having more.

But you can do it, even if wanting less seems like an insurmountable task.

3 Steps to Wanting Less

This basic 3-step strategy is all about wanting less and getting the most out of your life.

Step 1: Spend time with yourself

No, spending time by yourself is not the same as being lonely. Spending time alone helps you center yourself and understand who you really are. It is a beautiful and awakening practice.

Driven by superficial desires, we often gravitate toward extravagant things, including expensive digital tools, gadgets, and electronics.

Being alone with yourself helps you to know who you really are. The more you know yourself, the better you understand what your heart and mind truly desire.

Here's what you need to do:

Make a commitment to spend some time with yourself every day. It could be as little as 10 minutes, but make sure it happens.

Start the day with the specific intention of learning more about yourself and spending quality time with yourself.

Dedicate 10 to 60 minutes of your day to spending time with yourself. If you can spare 10 to 20 minutes at a time, try to do this twice a day.

During this time, try not to use any digital device, tool, software, app, game, or even digital data: be with yourself and explore your thoughts.

You may occasionally engage in activities that make you happy and peaceful or fun, such as cycling, painting, sculpting, listening to music, etc. But be sure to spend at least 2 or 3 of these "me-time" sessions exploring your thoughts and desires.

Once you start making time for yourself, you will find it easy to focus on your thoughts and desire less, which is the essence of Step 2.

Step 2: Explore and Understand Your Thoughts and Desires

The only way to truly want less is to understand what wanting more does to you.

If you fully understood the dangers of a disease, you would naturally avoid its triggers, right?

Similarly, if you fully understood how disastrous it is to want more, including wanting more digital stuff, you wouldn't want to hoard digital stuff. That only happens when you sit with your thoughts and peacefully observe them.

Yes, that's exactly why the first step was to spend quality time with yourself so that you learn to be comfortable in your presence and quietly observe your thoughts.

The key here is to quietly observe your thoughts without judgment, accepting them as they come so that you can analyze them without attaching too much meaning and drama to them.

When you evaluate thoughts without bias, you understand them better, which allows you to draw better conclusions.

Once you've spent time with yourself, here's what you really need to do:

Think about why you hoard digital devices.

Observe yourself for a while. Do you have a pattern of buying digital devices? How often do you buy these devices and gadgets? If you don't buy them often, think about all the devices and gadgets you have that you don't want to throw away. This includes all those old chargers, cables, and cords.

Also, think about why you keep saving pictures, files, and documents. Why do you think you cannot delete these files and keep saving more data?

Similarly, think about your behavior when it comes to apps and tools. How often do you use social media apps, games, and tools? And why do you use them? What compels you to spend hours using them and what keeps you engaged?

Think about each of these in turn. If you are thinking about digital devices, think about them in one session and then think about digital data in another session. It is important to get complete clarity on one aspect before moving on to the next.

If a particular aspect deserves more than one sitting, spend more time on it. Also, there is no hard and fast rule that says you must devote only one thinking session to an aspect. You can spend as much or as little time on each area as you wish.

Be sure to write down your thoughts or record yourself talking about them. A recording is better because it gives you a better sense of how you react to digital clutter.

Remember that you need to be very non-judgmental and accepting throughout this process. For example, if you realize that you are glued to social media because you need attention, accept it instead of being hard on yourself. Write: *"I often feel the need to seek attention, which draws me to social media."*

At the same time, try to dig deep into where this need comes from. This will help you find the root cause of the problem.

As you delve into your thoughts and discover how you behave around digital clutter, you will understand certain patterns of behavior. Now you need to move on to step 3.

Step 3: Understand How It Takes Away The Joy From Your Life, And Make Conscious Efforts To Want Less

Once you know how and why you behave a certain way, you are ready to take the plunge and make the behavioral change you have been wanting to make for a long time.

In this case, it is training yourself to want less digital clutter in your life.

Now that you have spent time with yourself and quietly observed your thoughts, you are more aware of your relationship with your digital devices and data.

The next step is to understand how your behaviors are taking joy out of your life so you can do something about it.

Get out your journal, and in your next "me time" session, go through any journal entry you would like to explore.

Whatever entry you are exploring, consider how that particular thing is keeping you from living a worthwhile life.

For example, if you are working on why you keep unnecessary cell phones and old chargers, think about how this behavior clutters your life and keeps you from being peaceful and happy. The phones and chargers take up drawer space that could otherwise be used for other things, such as storing books that you enjoy more.

Also, keeping them means you have to clean them, which adds to your stress. After you get rid of them, you have an empty, clean drawer and less clutter - and less stress.

Similarly, consider how spending less time on online games and deleting social media apps would restore sanity to your life. You can then invest the time saved in enjoyable activities. Perhaps you could learn a skill like playing the guitar-or something else you have always wanted to do.

Maybe you could spend time planting a vegetable garden that you enjoy. Think of ways to make time for what you really want to do, rather than what you do out of superficial desires and compulsions.

As you begin to figure out the reasons behind your need to want more digital clutter and all the things that weigh you down, begin to make conscious efforts to break free from this madness. These efforts don't have to be big. This is just the beginning; keep it simple and manageable.

Start by telling yourself: "I want less clutter and digital stuff in my life, and I am making a conscious effort to prove it." Say this out loud ten times. Write it down to reinforce your commitment.

Then remove just one cable, charger, or piece of digital data from your digital universe. For example, delete a picture you have been hoarding for a while. Once you do this, tune into your feelings and notice how you feel.

Each day take one small step to remove digital clutter from your life and desire less. You can either eliminate some clutter or stop inviting more digital clutter into your life.

If you want to do the latter, it is important to make saying no a habit in your life. If a friend invites you to like a Facebook page, say "no" in your head and decline the request.

Think about how it will clutter your news feed with unnecessary posts, making you feel overwhelmed and stressed. Similarly, if someone offers you a free software tool, don't accept it if you're not going to use it. This will help you want less, because it ensures that you're not inviting things that don't add real value to your life.

Notice all these small actions you take every day to manage your digital wants and practice digital minimalism. Reflect on your observations and review the journal entries regularly. As you track your performance, make positive changes to fine-tune your behavior. Perhaps you could not throw away your old tablet a month after buying a new one.

Once you acknowledge this behavior, reflect on the reason for the tendency and then take steps to overcome it. Maybe you are slipping into a relapse and need to review your reasons for wanting to get rid of digital clutter and become a digital minimalist. Reignite your motivation and make a fresh start.

These three steps can lead to a very happy and fulfilling life. They can bring a lot of convenience and comfort to your life, provided you practice them religiously and stick to them. They must also exist in a cycle.

This cycle must continue in an infinite loop for actual results to manifest in your life. You must spend time with yourself, reflect on your thoughts, and try to want less and eliminate clutter from your life. This is the only way it works.

To further strengthen this journey, shift your focus to all that truly brings meaning to your life.

The next chapter will teach you how to **focus on what really matters**.

Chapter 11: How to Focus on What Matters

"Always remember your focus determines your reality." —**George Lucas**

What you focus on shapes your mindset. Your mindset influences your thought process, and your thought process largely determines your attitude, behavior, and actions.

Therefore, what you focus on consistently contributes to your life choices and the overall shape and quality of your life.

To live a worthwhile life, you must straighten out your sense of focus and fixate on what is truly important to you.

A rudimentary step in doing this is to spend time with yourself, become more aware of your needs, understand what your digital life means to you, better assess your digital needs, and then focus on what really matters.

Since we covered this part in detail in the previous chapter, let's focus on some more golden tips and tricks you can use to start focusing on the things that matter most to you.

Change your perspective on technology

The modern age has somehow made us all "slaves" to technology. Because we often have at least one technological device in our hands, we have surrendered to technology. Whether we need to find a place, talk to someone, meet, find a client, socialize, or entertain ourselves, we look up to some technological medium to do the trick.

There is no denying the ease and convenience that technology brings to our lives. However, it is also important to remember that using technology for everything gives it the power to control us. It should be the other way around: we should control technology.

To start focusing on the things that are important to you, you need to shift your perspective on technology.

Instead of thinking of technology as something you need all the time and cannot do without, think of it more as a facilitating tool that helps you do your life and work better, not something that runs your life.

Here are some ideas to help you make this shift:

- Write down your views on each digital medium and tool and what it means to you.

- Be honest as you write down your thoughts.

- When you are finished, read your perspective aloud.

Now think about what it should actually mean to you. For example, if you only connect with friends through social media and rarely see them in person, you need to change how you use social media. Ideally, it should be a medium for connecting with people you know, not the only forum for socializing.

Now write, "I am working on changing my beliefs about digital tools, devices, and data and will only use them as a facilitative tool."

Read this out loud about ten times and write it down as you say it.

Review this statement every day. It will motivate you to stick with what you have decided to focus on and change. In addition, every time you begin to lean more toward a digital medium, tool, device, or data, think about how you are working to change your perspective.

With this approach, you will gradually succeed in changing your view of and addiction to digital media.

Once you change your perspective on it for the better, you will naturally focus on anything that truly brings you joy.

Use technology to facilitate your conversations

Once you start looking at technology differently, you need to use it differently.

Instead of letting digital tools and devices drive all your conversations and meetings, use them to facilitate them.

Face-to-face meetings with friends, contacts, business associates, employees, partners, vendors, and the like are always better than digital interactions. Since you are determined to focus on the right things in life, it is crucial to focus on the people involved.

When you meet with a potential client, you have a better chance of connecting with them and closing the deal in person rather than virtually.

No matter what the purpose of the meeting, try to bring the element of actual connection into it.

Here's what Cal Newport, author and digital decluttering expert, suggests:

When possible and manageable, have face-to-face meetings with your networks, friends, business partners, team members, etc. If a daily meeting is not possible, have it at least two to three times or at least once a week.

If your team works remotely or you cannot meet in person regularly with social and professional contacts, colleagues, vendors, etc., use video conferencing. Avoid text-only conversations and have them on a video call. This allows you to see each other face to face, understand each other's expressions, and establish real, direct communication.

For times when video chats are not possible, switch to phone calls. Hearing another person's voice gives you a sense of real human connection and bridges the gap between you and a coworker or friend.

Try these hacks, and also try to be available to friends, contacts, and networks when they want to meet with you in person.

Stop Clicking Like on Social Media

This may come as a big surprise to you, but according to Newport's research, responding to and commenting on social media posts is like slow poison.

The "like" button on Facebook is like an addictive slot machine that compels you to keep engaging with posts. The more you do it, the stronger the urge to scroll down and like more posts. Stop using this feature immediately.

To gain more control over how you allow digital media, especially social media, to control you, you need to stop liking posts.

Whenever your finger moves toward the "Like" button on Facebook, the "heart" reaction on Instagram, or similar buttons on other social media platforms, say "NO" out loud and move your finger away. Do this consciously for a few days and you'll master it.

Start the Attention Resistance

Digital media, especially social media, is an attention grab. You struggle to focus on the right things in life because of all the other distractions.

To start acting smarter, here are some ways to resist distraction:

Evaluate all the different apps, games, and other technological tools on your phone and laptop.

Keep only 3 to 5 of the most important ones, especially those related to work, personal life, finances, or anything else, but be careful not to keep more than 5 of the apps and tools.

Delete everything else. For example, delete the Facebook app that you don't use for anything other than connecting with people, checking your news feed, and buying stuff. You can still use Facebook on the web. Because using Facebook Web is a slightly less convenient option than using a phone, your use of the social media platform will automatically decrease when you switch to the web-based version.

Similarly, delete all other apps.

Also, make your devices single-purpose. For example, if you need to write a proposal right now without emailing it, turn off the WiFi on your laptop and write only in Word or Notepad. If you are working on your laptop, turn off the WiFi on your cell phone so that you are only using it to make and receive phone calls.

As you work through these guidelines, you will stop relying on digital media for everything and use it very purposefully.

Focus on enjoying the actual activities of life

Many of us complain about how little time we have for ourselves. While we complain, we often fail to realize that we waste a lot of time doing nothing but dancing to the tune of digital media.

Scrolling through the newsfeed or playing a game may seem like it only takes 10 minutes, but when you combine those little chunks of 5 and 10 minutes, you easily get a couple of hours. Used properly, those hours can add a lot of joy to your life.

Here is how to stop it:

Find those little chunks of time you spend aimlessly on digital media, doing nothing productive or meaningful.

Limit your use of digital technologies in those time slots, and combine those time slots into chunks of 30 minutes, 60 minutes, and so on.

Next, think about the different activities you want to do in the free time you just created, such as dancing, sculpting, listening to music, doing yoga, swimming, etc.

Create time for each activity you want to do, depending on how much time you need. For example, if you have created a 3 hour free time slot that you would otherwise spend on social media and Netflix, you can use those 3 hours for two or even more activities that you enjoy, such as biking and long walks.

The idea is to spend time doing leisurely activities that make you feel connected and satisfied with your life.

Use technology to feel how you want to feel.

In his book *Digital Minimalism*, **Cal Newport** talks about how we need to use technology according to our needs and how we want to feel. You can do that if you see yourself as controlling the technology, not the other way around.

Here's how to do it:

Ask yourself how technology and digital media make you feel in life. If it makes you feel chaotic and stressed, ask yourself why. Asking "why" digs into the matter and leads you to the real reason. Maybe it stresses you out because it makes you compare yourself to others.

Once you have identified the times and reasons that digital technologies are not helping you to feel the way you want, think about how you want to feel.

Write down these feelings and emotions in your journal; for example, you can write down happiness, peace, connection, etc.

Now think about the times you have gotten those feelings and emotions from your social media use. For example, if you want to feel a deep sense of connection with your family, think about the time you had a lively video chat and how it made you feel deeply connected. Similarly, if you want to feel a sense of freedom, think about how the GPS in your car gives you that feeling.

Think about the positive aspects of digital technologies and use them to fuel your gratitude. Practice this technique whenever digital media overwhelms you or does not make you feel the right way. Some examples include:

If you run an online business, think about how technology makes it easier for you to make a living, add value to people's lives, and be your own boss.

If you are a curious person with a thirst for knowledge, think about how the Internet quenches that thirst and puts knowledge at your fingertips.

If you love to write, focus on how a blog allows you to pursue your passion.

If you have always wanted to learn to play the piano and have been able to do so through YouTube tutorials, think about how YouTube has taught you an important skill.

The idea is not to make you feel awed by digital technologies, which might indirectly make you feel indebted to them.

The goal is to understand that you can turn things around and use digital technologies to feel how you want to feel.

Make it about you and your loved ones

Life is meant to be lived, not endured. The sooner you understand this valid point in life, the better. But how can we truly live and enjoy our lives? By focusing on yourself and your loved ones.

Make it a must to make time for yourself and your loved ones in your daily routine.

Spend some time each day with family members who live with you.

When spending time with loved ones, turn off your digital devices and make the time about them.

Engage in fun activities with your loved ones, such as picnics, movie nights, coloring, etc.

Every time you feel the urge to use digital technology, ask yourself if there is a good reason for it. If the answer is no, which is probably the case, consider your needs and priorities and choose them. For example, you may have signed up for a writing class, but you really want to watch videos on YouTube. Consider your real needs and use that reason to motivate yourself to attend the class.

As you work on all of these strategies, make a point of recording your daily performance in your journal. Make sure you also check in regularly to track your performance and progress.

Make changes to your life and routine based on the journal report. In addition, consider regular digital cleansing and learn how to avoid relapse.

Chapter 12: How to Avoid Digital Hoarding Relapse

"Digital minimalism definitely does not reject the innovations of the internet age, but instead rejects the way so many people currently engage with these tools."
—Cal Newport

Digital minimalism never asks you to shun technology. It simply teaches you to limit your use of it to the extent that you control it and are in charge.

If you are working on the strategies discussed in this book, I assume you have already begun your digital minimalism journey. You may have gotten rid of many of your unnecessary gadgets, deleted some of your applications, and tossed a lot of data from your computer into the digital trash.

In the process, you may have felt the urge to hoard digital data again.

Maybe you felt it when you saw your friend playing a new game online that seemed very addictive.

Maybe you overheard your coworkers talking about a new Instagram update that compelled you to reinstall the app and spend hours on it again.

Whatever the case, you've probably experienced a time when you almost slipped into a relapse, or maybe you actually did.

If the latter situation resonates with you, that's okay. It happens to the best of us.

The best thing to do is to have a good plan to try, experiment with, tweak, and use to block out your digital hoarding urges.

Fortunately, if you haven't slipped into a digital hoarding relapse yet, you probably won't, especially after reading the invaluable tips below.

Here are some strategies guaranteed to help you avoid a digital hoarding relapse, saving you time, energy, and sanity.

Notice the triggers

There is always one thing, or perhaps a cluster of factors, that triggers a particular behavior. The same is true for relapse.

If you are concerned that you may be having a digital hoarding relapse, or that you may be slipping into one, it is time to notice the triggers that may be causing this behavior.

Pay attention to your behavior and think about the different activities you engage in.

Do you spend a lot of time with certain people who use digital media excessively? Maybe your company has started a new project, and because you are in charge of it, you have to spend more time online, which somehow triggered your relapse.

Also, think about the places where you hang out the most. Maybe there is some social media-related wall art in your office that brings back old memories and makes you think about using it again/more.

Also, think about your mood and feelings. Have you gone through a monumental change or event in your life, perhaps a transition that has affected you deeply and left a mark on your mind? Many of us turn to social media, Netflix, and various digital tools and gadgets to manage stress and entertain ourselves.

If you are going through a rough patch in your life, this may be a trigger or one of the triggers that pushes you into a relapse of digital hoarding.

Once you have identified the various factors that may be triggering your digital hoarding relapse, write them down and observe your behavior closely for 5 to 7 days.

Notice how you behave in different situations, with different people, at different times, and when you experience different emotions.

Review these journal entries regularly to better understand your behavior.

Once you do, learn to manage these triggers effectively.

Managing the triggers

Getting a better handle on your triggers gives you more control over them and their effect on you.

Now that you know the various factors that can disrupt your digital minimalism routine, it is time to put them on a leash.

Start by gradually making some positive changes to your environment. If you find yourself in a room full of gadgets, digital electronics, or anything that reminds you of your old digital life, change it. Maybe you can take down that Facebook poster on your closet door. Maybe you need to take that TV screen out of your office so you can stop binge-watching Netflix shows.

Second, avoid hanging out with people who trigger your digital hoarding relapse. If certain friends still cannot control their digital data usage, meet with them occasionally.

Also, pay attention to your mood and look for ways to relieve the stress you absorb during the day. Learn to sit with your emotions and watch them carefully to understand what they are trying to tell you about yourself.

Once you have some answers, reflect on them and take appropriate action to resolve them. For example, if you are experiencing chronic sadness after a breakup, you may need to vent to a friend and then connect with more friends. Do this instead of spending hours on social media.

Create an action plan to manage your various triggers.

First, write down all your triggers and how they affect you in your journal.

Next, think of different ways to deal with them. Be creative and create more than one approach to managing each trigger. For example, if being around a certain friend causes you to hoard digital data, don't just avoid that particular friend. You may not be able to avoid being around that person, and you may need to try another hack, such as engaging in an immersive activity that takes your mind off digital hoarding.

Try out the different hacks and strategies you have come up with and see which ones work best.

Your action plan should now include a mix of the most effective strategies. That way, whenever you implement them, they will yield positive results.

Start working on these techniques and you'll soon have your triggers under control.

Keep a Commitment Reminder

We have certain keepsakes, mementos, and objects that remind us of certain events, memories, or things. Every time we look at these objects, we are reminded of the events associated with them.

It would be helpful to create something that reminds you of your commitment to digital minimalism. Let's call it your "commitment reminder," something that makes you think about your commitment to a particular goal.

Every time you look at this object, you will think of your commitment to practicing digital minimalism and feel motivated to keep it.

Think of any object you would like to associate with your digital minimalism journey, or anything that makes you feel better about it. It could be a mini-sculpture of a dove, maybe a painting with a big "no" symbol printed on various digital tools and devices, or anything else.

Take this item and place it in a particular corner or area of your room or house where you like to spend most of your time, or perhaps a place where you like to sit and think with clarity.

Each time you feel that your triggers are strongly affecting you, spend some time in front of your commitment reminder and think about what it means to you.

You will find yourself remembering all the different feelings it brings to digital minimalism, which will make you feel inclined to practice it sincerely.

You can also write down how your commitment reminder makes you feel to further solidify these feelings.

Practice mindfulness breathing meditation regularly

We often lose sight of what we really want in life. As a result, our thinking becomes clouded. As a result, we cannot focus on what is really important to us, and we become distracted. That's when we're likely to slip into a digital hoarding relapse.

Maybe you just went to a party where everyone had the latest iPhone, or where everyone was playing games on the latest Nintendo Switch.

Of course, being around such influences is likely to get to you. As a result, you may allow the triggers to set off your digital hoarding relapse.

A good way to prevent this is to keep your mind focused and clear, which is best done with mindfulness breathing meditation.

Mindfulness Breathing Meditation is a type of meditative practice that uses your breath as the object of concentration to get you to focus on it. As you learn to focus on your breath, you gradually become more focused on the present moment.

As a result, you begin to live in the moment, which helps you think with clarity and a newfound focus.

You find it easier to pay attention to the important things in life and avoid the unimportant. You gain more self-control, which automatically helps you manage your urges to relapse.

Here's how you can practice mindfulness breathing meditation to save yourself from a digital hoarding relapse:

First and foremost, find a quiet meditation spot. Expert meditators can safely meditate anywhere, even in the noisiest of places. However, since you are a beginner, you must understand that the start will not be straightforward.

You will struggle to maintain focus, which will not be easy. To make things manageable initially, sit somewhere peaceful to ensure you don't have to battle distracting thoughts and can focus better on your breath and the present moment.

When you settle on the spot, sit comfortably in any pose you like. You could cross your legs, kneel on the ground, sit on a chair, or lie flat on the yoga mat or couch. It is better to opt for a sitting pose than a lying one because the latter is likely to make you sleepy.

After settling down, close your eyes to ensure you do not get carried away by any sight in the environment. You can also open your eyes.

Place your hands on your thighs or right next to them.

Think of anything calming that relaxes you and focus on that memory or thought for a few moments.

When you feel re-centered, gently bring your attention to your breath.

Start observing your in-breath, aka inhalation. Observing it means very calmly watching the air enter and circulate in your body.

Remember to inhale through your nose and breathe in your normal, natural manner.

As the air moves around your body, observe it keenly and focus on how your abdomen inflates. Be as involved in the body movements as possible.

After your breath has completed its round and is about to exit your body, prepare to exhale through your mouth.

Exhale in your natural manner; no need to prolong your out-breath purposefully.

Just observe the out-breath and try to be as united with it as much as possible.

Keep going with these cycles for about 2 minutes. If 2 minutes feel too overwhelming initially, go for a round of 1 minute.

During this time, expect some distractions to happen. You may wander off in thought and start thinking about something else. Perhaps the chirping birds outside catch your attention, or maybe you start thinking of your meeting due in three hours.

Whatever the distraction might be, it is likely to disrupt you. Distractions are okay and part of the process. You are a novice, and this happens to even experts many times.

When a distracting phase occurs, acknowledge that you got lost in thought and accept it.

At that very point, take a deep breath, re-center yourself and re-align your attention back to your breath.

Count your breath with one full breath (one in-breath + one out-breath) = 1, the next full breath is 2, and so on until you reach 10, and start over from 1 again.

You may have to repeat the previous two steps many times until you gather complete control over your thoughts.

After 1 or 2 minutes of meditation, gently open your eyes and bring your awareness back to your present environment. Take some time to settle yourself into reality. Once you feel okay, think of how you feel.

The very first meditative session may not be as refreshing and calming as you would have expected. That may be due to the distracting thoughts that would have disturbed you all that while. Once again, it is okay to experience that.

What's important is that you must not give up on the practice: stick to it. Go ahead and practice it consistently for at least a week. You will notice a positive difference in how you feel about the practice and your thinking ability in different situations.

Next, gradually increase the duration of the meditative practice so you meditate for slightly longer time durations. Try to take your practice up to 15 minutes a stretch.

Meanwhile, use it to think about digital minimalism and how to stay strong while avoiding the triggers that pull you towards relapse. The more you meditate, the stronger your willpower will become, and the easier it will be to prevent a digital hoarding relapse.

Entice Yourself with an Attractive Reward

Rewards work like a charm.

Remember how we used to actively study for our exams or do anything else with an attached reward? You need to apply the same principle here.

Entice yourself with a reward to stay dedicated to your digital minimalism commitment and ensure you do not fall into the relapse trap.

Think of anything you will enjoy as a reward, perhaps a lunch treat, a movie night with friends, a new watch you have been eyeing, or anything else you find quite attractive and rewarding.

Peg it to a certain digital minimalism goal, such as not using social media for a week, not storing digital data for a month, or anything else.

Make sure to write down your goal and the reward clearly in your journal to ensure full clarity of the two.

Write down a starting and ending date for the goal to make it more exciting, and then start following your journey.

Chapter 13: Make Your Clutter-Free Shrine

Like a commitment reminder, a clutter-free shrine keeps you connected to your goal of living a minimalist digital life.

A clutter-free shrine serves as a clean, peaceful space where you can sit, meditate, reflect on your minimalist values, and feel motivated to live the life you want to live.

Of course, when you are in such a place and reflect on what digital minimalism means to you, how it adds value to your life, and why you need to let go of digital hoarding, you get a newfound motivation to stay true to your goal and achieve it.

The journey to becoming a complete digital minimalist is arduous. The journey is not impossible; it can be lived and mastered.

Like everything else in life, you will encounter some problems along the way. When your temptations hit you hard and it becomes quite difficult to control them, spending some time at your clutter-free shrine will do wonders to rekindle your values and help you gain the strength not to go astray.

Here's what you need to do to set up your shrine:

Find a nice place in your bedroom or home to set up your uncluttered shrine. It could be an area in your living room, bedroom, or garden.

Place a table there and add an item or two that reminds you of your digital minimalism goal. Perhaps you have a lamp, a Buddha statue, a bonsai tree, or something else that brings you feelings of peace.

You can also place your digital minimalism journal and other things such as notes, pictures, or anything else you use to fuel your motivation to live a minimalist digital life.

Please make sure the space and everything around it is clean and uncluttered.

You must hang out at your shrine for 15 minutes every day - this is a MUST!

When you do, clean the shrine and see if any clutter has crept in. If it has, clear the area.

Write down your feelings about digital minimalism and digital hoarding relapse after spending time in your clutter-free shrine.

Try this strategy for a week and see how you feel. You will probably feel more enthusiastic about your goal and more determined to stick with it.

Have an accountability buddy

Accountability is an important virtue that makes you responsible for your actions and decisions. When you learn to be accountable for your actions, you take extra care to act in a certain way.

One of the many effective ways to become accountable is to have an accountability buddy for whatever goal you want to be accountable for or achieve.

Similarly, in this scenario, you can have an accountability buddy to keep you on the path of digital minimalism and ensure that you do not slip back into digital hoarding.

An accountability buddy checks your performance, helps you analyze your daily activities, and acts as a regulator to ensure that you stay on track and do not stray from your goal.

Of course, with constant reminders of your goal and an objective assessment of your performance, you will find it easy to stay on track.

Here's how to find an accountability buddy and use this approach to avoid a relapse into digital hoarding.

Spread the word about a friend interested in being your accountability buddy. You can share a post on social media, let your close friends know you are looking for an accountability buddy, and even spread the word in any support group you are a part of.

Be sure to be specific about what you are looking for in an accountability buddy. In this case, indicate that you are looking for an accountability buddy to help you overcome the urge to relapse into digital hoarding.

Once you get some responses or interest from people who want to be your accountability buddy, connect with them and see if you can build a trusting relationship. It's important to trust your accountability buddy, or you won't take their advice and feedback seriously.

Once you have found someone you consider trustworthy and vice versa, share your daily routine with that person and establish a mode of accountability. You can share your daily progress with your buddy through text messages, phone calls, video chat, or media.

If the two of you can meet daily - or even a few times a week - schedule it. Since the goal is to avoid digital media, face-to-face accountability is best. However, it is also understandable that meeting daily may be difficult. In that case, include some element of face-to-face interaction and try to hold your meetings via video conference. If this is not possible on a regular basis, use phone calls and texting as a last resort.

Be honest with your accountability buddy about your digital media use. This person may not be around 24/7 to constantly monitor you. So, of course, they cannot always see what you are doing. If you keep a journal or record yourself talking about your digital media behavior, share it openly with your accountability buddy.

Also, if you are going through a major change, transition, or phase in your life, such as a breakup, job loss, business problems, financial crisis, personal problems, or anything else that has caused a massive change in your mood, behavior, and attitude, tell your buddy.

Your honesty will give your buddy a clear picture of your current situation and your tendency toward digital hoarding. Only with the right information can your accountability partner develop the right plan and strategies to help you stay strong and control the urge to give in to your temptations.

You may find that your accountability partner is strict at times. Any time your accountability partner feels a bit harsh or disciplinary, understand that it is for your good. However, if you do not like your accountability buddy's demeanor, tone, attitude, disciplinary approach, or anything else, bring it to their attention. The two of you must communicate openly and honestly, or it will be difficult for you to gain each other's trust and help each other.

It is also a good idea to find someone else who is trying to practice digital decluttering; you can be that person's accountability buddy, and they can return the favor. This approach makes things more manageable and smoother for both of you. It also gives both of you an equal opportunity to discipline each other, and you won't feel upset when the person sets certain rules for you.

Start working on finding your accountability buddy right away so that you can get right down to business and take steps to achieve your goals.

These steps can seriously change your life for the better. They are not just strategies; they are life-changing approaches that can improve your quality of life and keep relapse at bay.

Let's move on to the next chapter and discuss some more pro tips to make sure you stay safe from digital clutter.

Chapter 14: Further Protection Against Digital Clutter

"You are the average of the five people you spend the most time with." — **Jim Rohn**

Digital clutter can get out of hand very quickly. At this point, we have established that for sure. Of course, it is best to have as much protection against it as possible.

In this chapter, we will look at other tips and tricks that can help you strengthen your digital clutter shield and live a better, more minimalist digital life.

Be Careful About the People You Hang Out With

No quote has ever hit the nail on the head.

The people you hang out with directly influence your personality, your mood, your attitude, your decisions, your actions, and therefore your life. Therefore, it is best to be careful about who you let into your space.

As you work toward becoming a digital minimalist and enjoy the journey, surround yourself with people who appreciate your goal, resonate with it, and encourage you to stick with it.

Such people will have your back and inspire you to follow your mission and continue to improve your decluttering game.

On the other hand, if you hang out with digital hoarders, you are likely to revert to your old ways. Soon your digital devices will be overflowing with tons of data, making it difficult for you to keep track.

The moral of the story is that you should spend time with digital minimalists, or if not exactly digital minimalists, at least those who understand the cause and encourage you to stay true to it.

Identify the different influences in your social circle, those you hang out with most, those who are explicitly hoarders, and those who tend to be hoarders.

Make a list of these people.

While you do not need to cut ties with all of them, especially if you have a close bond with some of them, you do need to limit your interaction with some of them, especially those who tend to influence you a lot.

To distance yourself from the hoarders, you can meet with them occasionally, not take their calls often, and not spend too much time with them.

Also, start saying "no" to their suggestions and advice. If a friend suggests you try an app, say no. This may seem challenging at first, but it will get easier after you do it a few times.

In the meantime, look for digital minimalists in your social circle who can inspire you. If your current social circle is devoid of such people, spread the word that you are looking for some nice people of this sort to learn from. Soon you will be exposed to some cool influences and learn a lot.

Keeping a journal of your social contacts and how they influence you is a good way to make sure you stay on track.

Become process oriented

The process is what gets you there. So it is important to enjoy the journey rather than fixate on the destination.

To become a true digital minimalist who truly seeks the joy of decluttering your digital universe, you need to start enjoying the daily process that makes magic happen in your life. What's magic here? Digital decluttering, of course!

Digital minimalism experts and self-help gurus recommend that we all become process-oriented in order to enjoy the process of achieving our goals.

When we get too goal-oriented, we often get too worked up about it. If we falter or make a mistake, we fear slipping away from our goal. In this case, our fear consumes us and prevents us from functioning optimally. As a result, we begin to move away from our goal instead of moving toward it.

We can solve this problem by becoming process-oriented!

Here's how to do this trick:

Every time you clean up something digitally, whether it's deleting a file or throwing away a digital device, take note of your feelings. Notice how relieved and peaceful you feel.

Write down these feelings or record yourself talking about them.

Feed yourself encouragement for a job well done, and notice the space you have created in both your digital devices and your mind by getting rid of clutter.

Every time you say no to a file, document, or other digital item, feel good about not accepting something that would only add more chaos and stress to your life.

Spend 5 minutes at your clutter-free shrine and reflect on your feelings. Think about how good you feel living a minimalist digital life and the immense value it adds to your life.

When you go on a digital or social media detox, spend more time doing things you enjoy and hanging out with people you really care about.

Write about and reflect on your daily digital activities and whereabouts. Figure out where you went wrong and where you went right. Take your strengths, weaknesses, mistakes, failures, and successes and learn to use them wisely.

As you work on all these guidelines, you will become more immersed in the process that will lead you to the end goal and make you truly enjoy it.

Have Regular Digital Purges

Digital detox now needs to be a regular part of your life. You need to go on a digital cleanse every now and then.

Just as health experts advise us to go on a detox diet or drink detox water to cleanse the body of impurities, toxins, and harmful chemicals, you need a regular digital detox to cleanse your system of digital impurities.

Start with a social media detox and avoid using social media platforms for about 30 minutes.

Once you have done this once, try it again the next day.

Slowly increase the length of your social media detox to a few hours.

If you can avoid using social media for an hour, do a full digital detox for a few hours. This includes not using your phone, laptop, internet, or other digital devices for a few hours. You can start with 30 minutes and gradually build up to 3 to 4 hours.

Practice digital detox at least twice a week.

Once you get the hang of it, move on to practicing for at least 12 hours.

Your next milestone is to go on a digital cleanse for a full day. It may feel a little tricky and challenging at first, but you will begin to enjoy it if you focus on enjoying the process.

Make these detoxes and purges a regular part of your life.

To increase the fun and excitement, ask friends and family to join you. For example, you can do a one-day digital detox with your family, where you keep each other in check.

Print out your "whys

If you haven't considered why you want to become a digital minimalist, it's time to dig deep and think about this important topic.

Your whys are the reasons that complement a particular movement, goal, or transition in your life.

Say you want to lose weight to become healthier; getting healthy is your reason here.

You want to earn more money to become financially independent; financial independence is your why here.

You want to eat organic food and control your diet to control your blood pressure; controlling your blood pressure is your why.

When you have a strong reason to support your goal, you automatically become more committed to it and feel willing to go the extra mile to achieve it because you know you have something meaningful to look forward to.

Similarly, in this case, you need to have strong, compelling "whys" to complement your goal of becoming a digital minimalist. It's in your best interest to really think about it and find out why this thing means so much to you.

Once you have uncovered the real "whys" behind your desire to practice digital decluttering, you will realize the various ways in which digital hoarding has held you back.

Whenever your motivation falters or you feel like relapsing, a quick glance at your "whys" will reignite your enthusiasm and get you back on track.

Here's what you need to do:

Sit down in a peaceful and quiet place with your journal.

Think about what digital minimalism means to you and why you need to practice digital decluttering.

Write down all your reasons for wanting to detox, declutter, and become a digital minimalist.

Write different reasons and categories on different pages of your journal.

Now make several copies of these pages and place them in different parts of your home. One copy could go on the refrigerator, another on the bathroom mirror, one on the nightstand, another on the dining room table, and so on.

You could also turn one page of your Why's into a cool graphic and have it framed on a main wall in your house or bedroom. Perhaps you could write an affirmation for your digital minimalism, such as "I am a digital minimalist and I own it. You could then have it framed and hang it in a prominent place. Such affirmations help you stay connected to your goal.

In addition, as you work on your "why," chant some powerful digital minimalist affirmations every day. Affirmations are suggestions that you believe in; they rewire your brain to think the way you want.

Here are some affirmations to chant:

"I love decluttering my digital universe.

"Digital minimalism makes my life happy and peaceful.

"Digital minimalism adds value and meaning to my life.

"I declutter my digital spaces every day.

"I breathe out stress and breathe in peace.

"I let go of clutter in my mind and in my life.

"I enjoy getting rid of meaningless things from my life.

"I only keep things, data and information that I need.

"I am a digital minimalist and I love it.

"I am proud of my decision to become a digital minimalist.

Try these affirmations every day. Better yet, practice them while sitting at your clutter-free shrine.

These tips may seem simple, but if you practice them vehemently and religiously, you will quickly realize their power.

The more you practice them, the more you get used to them, the more you enjoy them, and the more they improve your overall well-being.

Conclusion

Thank you for believing in yourself and trusting in the power of this book.

You have definitely made a vital investment in yourself that will continue to repay itself repeatedly.

I hope you have found the value you were seeking and that you use this book wisely to turn your digital environment around for the best.

Remember, chaos is always just one click away...stay committed to cleaning your digital house on a regular basis and you will be happier working both online and offline.

All the best,

Scott Allan

"Your body is the temporary temple of your Spirit. What you keep around you in the extended temple of your home needs to change as you change and grow, so that it reflects who you are."

— **Karen Kingston**

About Scott Allan

Scott Allan is an international bestselling author of over 30 books published in 12 languages in the area of personal growth and self-development. He is the author of **Fail Big**, **Undefeated,** and **Do the Hard Things First**.

As a former corporate business trainer in Japan, and **Transformational Mindset Strategist**, Scott has invested over 10,000 hours of research and instructional coaching into the areas of self-mastery and leadership training.

With an unrelenting passion for teaching, building critical life skills, and inspiring people around the world to take charge of their lives, Scott Allan is committed to a path of **constant and never-ending self-improvement**.

Many of the success strategies and self-empowerment material that is reinventing lives around the world evolves from Scott Allan's 20 years of practice and teaching critical skills to corporate executives, individuals, and business owners.

You can connect with Scott at:

scottallan@scottallanpublishing.com

https://www.scottallanpublishing.com/

Scott Allan

"Master Your Life One Book at a Time."

[Subscribe]() to the weekly newsletter for actionable content and updates on future book releases from Scott Allan